THESE POEMS NEED HOMES
WHOSE IDEA WAS THIS ANYWAYS?

THESE POEMS NEED HOMES
WHOSE IDEA WAS THIS ANYWAYS?

Dominic "Flominic" Farrenkopf

Cover Image illustrated by Hannah Farrenkopf
Author photo by Wayne Wardwell

authorHOUSE®

AuthorHouse™ LLC
1663 Liberty Drive
Bloomington, IN 47403
www.authorhouse.com
Phone: 1-800-839-8640

Published by AuthorHouse   11/20/2013

ISBN: 978-1-4918-3750-4 (sc)
ISBN: 978-1-4918-3751-1 (e)

Library of Congress Control Number: 2013921526

TABLE OF CONTENTS

BONUS POEMS

DEDICATION

For Brian.
Who encouraged, supported, listened . . .
and whose idea this was anyways.

PREFACE

Dominic "Flominic" Farrenkopf has this strange idea that poetry ought to rhyme. Maybe he picked it up from that playwright of Stratford-upon-Avon, who, at the end of a particularly dramatic action, would abandon his blank verse for a rhyming couplet. But, whereas Shakespeare seemed always to be serious, Flominic is usually whimsical. Still, his light touch of an everyday scene does not mean there is not a lesson to be learned from the twist he inflicts on you at the end. These are verses to be enjoyed and chuckled over, and returned to from time to time. Flom has a quirky, creative energy not seen in many, and it is not limited to writing. He is constantly dreaming up ridiculous things for us residents at Sapphire Lutheran Homes. And it is these things which keep us ancients alive and kicking. I know you will enjoy what he is saying directly, as well as the hidden insights which pop up when you cogitate a while.

~Wayne Wardwell

I Wanna Know . . .

"Hey Flominic. Write some poems!"
That's what someone said.
"You'll have lots of fun rhyming
and that fun will spread!"

"People will enjoy them
and that is very true
plus it will give you
something quite useful to do."

So now I'll sit and rhyme
for the rest of my days.
I wanna know . . .
whose idea was this anyways!?

March 10, 2012

Crackers

I've got a frog in my throat,
and the cat's got my tongue.
There's bats in my belfry,
and I'm still so young!

I'm quiet as a mouse,
even though I want to monkey around.
But I'm too busy "scratchin' fleas"
like an old blue tick hound.

I have a Charlie horse in my leg,
and in my hair a cow-lick.
There's butterflies in my belly,
and I think I'm gonna be sick!

There's a bee in my bonnet,
and my ducky pond is just full of quackers.
I'm feeling kind of crabby.
Oh, why did I eat all those animal crackers!?

I wrote two poems for St. Patrick's Day in 2012. I wasn't sure which one to put in the paper. Sherry published them both.

March 17, 2012

My Pot Of Gold

Just this morning
in the fog and cold,
I found a leprechaun's
pot of gold.

I raced right on down
to the candy store,
and bought truffles
licorice and lots, lots more.

Jawbreakers, chewing gum,
candy bars and lollipops,
peppermint sticks, salt water taffy,
fudge and gumdrops.

At the soda fountain
I bought a chocolate sundae,
then washed it down
with a cherry milkshake right away.

Now as I walk slowly home
let the truth be told,
my stomach felt better . . .
before my pot of gold!

March 17, 2012

The Leprechaun

In Ireland, I asked a man,
how to make a wish come true.
He said, "Go catch a leprechaun,
that's all that you have to do."

"How do I catch one?"
I asked the chap.
"That's easy," said he
"build a leprechaun trap."

"Here's a list of what you'll need:
A length of rope, a bundle of sticks,
the gold ring from your right hand,
and a horseshoe to ward off his tricks."

"Get him a bunch of clover sprouts
and a peacock feather for his hat."
I got the things and set the trap
then down with the little man I sat.

I sang out the magic words
the man said the leprechaun would hear
then dove on the stick pile
where the little person would appear.

The sticks caved in, my ring vanished
and on this you can bet
as the little man danced away . . .
I wished we'd never met!

March 24, 2012

A Marvelous Thing

He sits in his desk
and starts to squirm
not unlike
a mud puddle worm.

She's anxious too
as she sits in her seat
swinging her legs
green galoshes on her feet.

The bell rings
he grabs his yellow kite
and runs outside
The wind is just right.

She leaps from her desk
to pick daffodils
then wades in puddles
for giggles and thrills.

He and his friends
start a mud ball war
slinging mud back and forth
to even the score.

She and her friends
get out the jump ropes
and for hopscotch weather
they have high hopes.

He's also feeling
rather silly and giddy
but sure won't admit
the girls all look pretty.

She watches the robins
and for birds building nests
and now the boys seem cute
and no longer pests.

They both run home
in a breeze that's nice and cool.
Their moms aren't surprised
they left their coats at school.

The cause of this behavior
is a marvelous thing.
The whole world is transformed . . .
when we welcome spring!

I quickly realized that writing my poems to correspond with seasons and holidays was a great idea.

The Broken Window

Don't be mad mom
or you either, pop
but a window got broke
out in the shop.

And speaking of things
that are getting broke
I should mention
gram's chest of solid oak.

I used the chest's lid
to put out a fire
that started in the trunk
on dad's spare tire.

When the lid didn't work
I threw on some dirt
but to put it out
I had to use my best shirt.

I had my best shirt on
when the policeman came
I wanted to look my best
to not tarnish our name.

I didn't want
to end up in jail
so I lit the gas
I had in a pail.

I thought that a roaring blaze
would distract the cop
that's when his bullet
broke the window in the shop.

I know that I
broke a lot of rules
and it's all because of . . .
April Fools!

Filled To The Brim

It has a pretty blue bird
building a nest
and three pink seashells
next to a treasure chest.

It's decorated with
leaves and strawberries
and glittering dew
on plump red cherries.

There's a little bush
with roses and thorns
and four white angels
blowing golden horns.

It has six fuzzy branches
of pussy willows
and a rainbow of ribbons
on cloud pillows.

It's covered with flowers
like blue bell and sweet pea,
tiger lily, daffodil
and white daisy.

There's two cinnamon sticks
and a bag of nutmeg spice
right next to a fuzzy rabbit
and seven baby mice.

It has a puddle duck
and a gaggle of geese
a milk cow, her calf
and a sheep with soft fleece.

How does gram keep her head up
with all that stuff on it?
It's amazing, cause that's one heavy . . .
Easter bonnet!

April 14, 2012

Puddle Jumper

I begin to smile
when it starts to rain.
But mom and dad act like
it's a great big pain.

My folks frown
when there's a thunder cloud.
But I hop up and down
and clap really loud.

They drag out their umbrellas
like it's a chore.
But when I hear it raining
I only want more.

I throw on my slicker
and rubber galoshes
then rush outside
for splashes and sploshes.

I never jump over
I hop right in.
Seeing the water fly
really makes me grin.

Through the muck
I stamp and stomp
and charge around
in my private swamp.

I make mud balls
and slosh around
I whoop and holler
and trample the ground.

Mom says it's not lady-like
and dad's car gets a dirty bumper.
But no matter what they say . . .
I love being a puddle jumper!

April 21, 2012

One Man's Trash

It's Saturday morning
and you ignore the words
in the newspaper that say:
"No early birds."

So at six a.m.
with cash in your hand
you head out the door
just like you planned.

The good ones
are all circled in red.
Go here first-
they just cleaned out their shed.

It says they have
tools and fishing tackle,
old tires, scaffolding,
and drywall spackle.

Let's go here because they have
china tea cups, dishes and antiques,
kitchen utensils, Tupperware
and a canoe that slightly leaks.

Up next is a multi-family
both indoor and out
bikes, games, books—stop here!
even though it's not on our route.

Looks mostly like yarn and thread
for a weaving loom
but I know this guy
and we can use his bathroom.

There's a big estate sale
right up the street.
Treadmill, knick knacks, toys
and a free parakeet.

They've got records on vinyl
a washer/dryer matching pair,
lamps, golf clubs, baby stroller
and gently used high chair.

Yes, for a few bucks
it will be my pleasure
to turn your old trash . . .
into my new treasure!

This poem was written with Arbor Day in mind. Can you tell?

April 28, 2012

Grab A Shovel

You will need two sturdy ones
for cool shade
and for the hammock
where you'll sip lemonade.

Childhood memories
are a marvelous thing
especially when they include
a tire swing.

Juicy cherries in the sun
or a fresh ripe peach.
You just might need a ladder
to help you reach.

Their blossoms in the spring
are fragrant, pink and white
and autumn's orange foliage
are torches burning bright.

A teenage boy
carves his true love's name
where as a young lad
he climbed the same.

What would Christmas be
without a festive wreath
or without an evergreen
with presents underneath?

You have to have them
to build your home
and for the paper
that holds this poem.

They are important
and if you agree
grab a shovel . . .
and plant a tree!

This poem ushered in the 2012 Farmer's Market held in Hamilton, Montana.

May 5, 2012

Plentiful Bounty

Everyone is welcome
to sample plentiful, local bounty
each Saturday, right next to
the museum of Ravalli County.

Let's all hope
the weather is sunny
and then stock up
on clover honey.

There are potted plants
and art work, you know.
When you get there
grab a hot espresso.

You can get ripe veggies
like corn and fresh picked peas.
Pack your puppy in your coat
because: "No dogs, please."

There are pastries available
like cream cheese pumpkin rolls.
You can find cinnamon buns
and hand-thrown pottery bowls.

Homemade bread is always nice
along with muffins and great fruit pies.
Jewelry, crafts, knitted blankets-
for a baby shower surprise.

Another fantastic find
around each bend
you can't help but bump
into a good friend.

So hop in your car
then find a place to park it
and take your family . . .
to the Farmer's Market!

May 12, 2012

It Was She

It was she who nursed me
and changed my nappy
we played Peek-A-Boo
which made us both happy.

It was she who held my hands
as I learned to walk
and helped me form my words
as I learned to talk.

It was she who was patient
even when I fussed
and made me PB and J
without any crust.

It was she who taught me
the golden rule
and calmed my fears
on my first day of school.

It was she who doctored
all of my bike wreck scars
and saw me go from toy soldiers
to girls and cars.

It was she who saw me
graduate with my class
and on my wedding day
toasted me with raised glass.

It was she who raised me
and now that I'm grown
it is she I call
each Sunday on the phone.

It is she who is truly
like no other
the one in my life . . .
I simply call "mother".

May 19, 2012

Kite

It's four feet high
and about three feet wide.
To assemble it
we did it outside.

The cross sticks are
Canadian maple
and held together
with a steel staple.

The fringe edging
makes a whistling sound
that you can still hear
even from the ground.

The string on the spool
is blackstone cord.
To cut it in two
you'd need a sword.

The tail is white
and eleven feet long.
It's made of canvas
so it's really strong.

It's bright cherry red
with a yellow stripe.
We just hope
it can live up to the hype.

The box says
it will easily fly
up to four hundred
soaring feet high.

Will it go that high?
We just don't know.
We have our kite . . .
but the wind won't blow!

May 26, 2012

Our Fallen

A common thread
for each and every age
are the fallen dead
from the wars we wage.

And each Memorial Day
we remember our lost
as we continually pray
we don't forget the cost.

They paid the ultimate price
when they answered the call
and they'd do it twice
if it bought freedom for all.

For when a soldier dies
on the battlefield of war
he closes his young eyes
never to open them anymore.

His medals for acts of valor
pass on to his brother
but won't remove the pallor
from the face of his mother.

We lose husbands and beaus
beloved fathers and sons
to lonely cemetery rows
from our opponent's guns.

We lose mothers and daughters
sisters too, in modern day
to war's dark, troubled waters
for now that's part of the way.

Even with tireless toil
all of the wars are the same
many don't return to home soil
and there's a grave with no name.

But hold on to those you knew
who we lost in the fight
who with hearts so pure and true
championed for what's right.

Each spring our eyes have tears
not just from the pollen
but because from past years . . .
we remember our fallen.

This poem was written for the graduating class of 2012. As I wrote this poem I couldn't help but remember what high school was like. I think that is one of my favorite thing about writing poems—going back and remembering how things were.

June 2, 2012

Cap And Gown Countdown

Your countdown started
on your first Freshman day
when your graduation
seemed so far away.

You huddled close
with all of your friends
and gaped at the halls
without any ends.

It wasn't long
and you knew your way around.
Looking back now
you sure covered lot's of ground.

Algebra One and Algebra Two
sandwiched Geometry
Biology, Physics, Pre-Calc
and of course—Chemistry.

Grammar, English Lit,
Composition and that's not all
vocab and spelling tests.
Thank goodness for study hall!

Art, Pottery, Weights,
Woodshop, Band and Drama
without these electives
you'd all be in trauma.

Foot-, Basket-, Soft-,
Volley—all these end with "ball"
Tennis, Speech, Track, Soccer
yes, you played them all.

Friday night lights,
Senior prom, Homecoming parade,
off campus lunch, Senior skip day
you had it made!

Your teachers, coaches and friends
you'll never forget
but you now look towards
what you haven't done yet.

So with caps thrown high
and your gowns unfurled
you're the class of Twenty-Twelve . . .
look out world!

After my annual "Give That Boy A Haircut" fundraiser, many people requested a hair do poem. Here it is!

June 9, 2012

Hair-do

Comb it over
or slick it back.
Part it down the middle
like a railroad track.

Throw in some gel
or better yet, lard.
Mix it in good
so it's stiff and hard.

Spike it up
or comb it down.
if it's grey
dye it black or brown.

Let it fall
over your eyes
or style it in the dark
for a nice surprise.

You can crimp
and you can curl
or wear piggy-tails
like a little girl.

Shave it off
or let it fall out.
If you want to save it
rub in oil of trout.

Make a braid
with three long strands.
Fasten it with
old rubber bands.

Or choose the one
I haven't said.
The classic, easy to style . . .
bed-head!

June 16, 2012

Fish Pond

He was the first one
to teach me to bait my hook
and could untangle a snag
with merely a look.

He would row so stealthily
out into the deep
and silently drop my line
where the big ones sleep.

He showed me exactly
when to start to reel
when the bobber dipped-
he could do it by feel.

Whenever I was reeling in
you can sure bet
he was always ready
and waiting with the net.

He would take out the hook
and then measure the fish
and joke about how
it wouldn't fit on my dish.

We would catch our limit
not a single one more
then with his strong arms
he would row us both to shore.

He'd build a fire
and fry the fish in the pan
while he carefully molded me
into a man.

As I look back
I'm thankful for the time I had
sitting, talking, bonding . . .
just fishing with my dad.

June 23, 2012

Sounds Good To Me

Tweet Tweet
Morning birds,
singing in the trees.

Shshsh
Hammock time,
in the afternoon breeze.

Woosh Woosh
Swing your way,
high up from the ground.

WHEeeeEEE
Spin circles,
on the merry-go-round.

Cring-Cring
Hurry!
The ice cream man is here.

Shlurp
Grape popsicle juice,
from ear to ear.

Chink-Chink
Run in,
the sprinkler outside.

Shleee
Or play for hours,
on the slip-n-slide.

Lap, Lap
Waves against,
the boat at the lake.

Sploosh
Tubing in the boat's,
foamy white wake.

Whump-Shloop
Sand from a bucket,
on the beach.

Fwlap
Your kite soars overhead,
out of reach.

Crack-Crunch
Peanuts for,
inning seven's stretch.

Shlap
A home-run ball in your mitt-
great catch!

Thump Thump
This watermelon's,
ripe indeed.

Spoot
How far away,
can you spit a seed?

Tink Tink
Ice cubes in,
your lemonade glass.

Hisss
Now light the barbecue's,
propane gas.

Vizz Vizz
Wings of a bird,
that's a hummer.

Ahhhh
How I do love . . .
the sounds of summer!

June 30, 2012

Independence Day

We could get up early
and head to Main Street.
For the parade
we would want a front row seat.

The floats will come by
dressed in red, white and blue
showing off the past
and how our country grew.

There's "George Washington
Crossing the Delaware"
and "Betsy Ross Sewing the Flag
with Great Care".

Ribbons will be passed later
at the bandstand
now for the picnic
that for a week's been planned.

Bread and butter sandwiches,
cold fried chicken,
potato salad . . .
but the clocks a' tickin'.

The food can wait!
The kids all take their places
for the three-legged
and gunny sack races.

Then back to the picnic tables
and here's why:
home-made ice cream
and freshly baked apple pie!

Later it's watermelon
and lemonade
as we listen to the band
in the cool shade.

The kids will dance with sparklers
on the lawn
while fireworks light the sky
when day is gone.

So let's get together
what do you say?
And have an old fashioned . . .
Independence Day!

People get married. Before they exchange their vows there are loads of things that must first be set in place. This poem lists them all.

July 7, 2012

Something Old, Something New

She finally met "Mr. Right"
their love's so true
so she got something borrowed
and got something blue.

She's making a guest list
and trying on dresses
wedding invitations
are hot off the presses.

Bride's maids and maid of honor
are hand selected
their secret honeymoon place
is well protected.

She's hired a planner
for the preparations.
For the church
she has flowers and decorations.

She's ordered a four tier
butter cream wedding cake
and reserved the great room
at the lodge by the lake.

The rehearsal dinner
will be a great event.
For it's reception
she orders an extra tent.

The photographer and DJ
are now both booked.
The caterer knows
the pig must be fully cooked.

And so she says,
"Everything's ready I suppose.
Now to figure out . . .
how to make that boy propose!"

These next two poems that appeared in July of 2012 were actually a double header. I felt that the poems were appropriate for this time of year, but just too short to run one at a time. Here they are:

July 14, 2012

A Dreadful Condition

It happens suddenly
when you least expect
kind of like a bit of
whiplash in the neck.

It's quite painful
and it will surprise you
just be glad that
it won't paralyze you.

It's face wrenching
like hot mustard spice
and you feel like
your head's in a vice.

Ice cream cones, popsicles, milk shakes
or anything else like these
can cause the dreadful condition
simply known as . . . brain freeze!

July 14, 2012

Shirt

She sneaked up behind
and dropped it in from the back
I hollered like a banshee
having a heart attack.

I leaped in the air
like a monkey out of a bag
I lost all of my breath
and began to choke and gag.

I whooped and hollered
like I was doing a war dance
or that there was a fire
down in my underpants.

I quickly threw myself
right down on the ground
like a fish out of water
I flopped around.

I finally got it out,
and although it doesn't hurt
there is absolutely nothing worse . . .
than ice down your shirt!

July 21, 2012

Big Sky Country

When you come to Big Sky country
cast a glance around,
a more beautiful creation
will never be found.

From the Sweet Grass Hills
to the rolling Prairie County,
the Golden Triangle
with it's wheat and grain bounty.

The Bob Marshall's wilds
Glacier and Yellowstone park,
the great chasms of the caverns
of Lewis and Clark.

The impressive lakes of Flathead,
Holland and Georgetown,
Kootenai and Big Creek
from the mountains—come pouring down.

The Big Hole, Gallatin,
Thompson and Ruby Rivers,
gazing at The Bob's Chinese Wall
will give you shivers.

Visit the Great Bear Paw Mountains
or the Grey Wolf Peak,
the Gates of the Mountains,
will make you feel quite meek.

Hike up Swan Creek,
Bridger Ridge or the Beehive Basin,
climb to Grinnell Glacier-
it will leave your heart racin'.

Many great places he's made
but between you and I,
when God wants to brag . . .
He paints us a Bitterroot Sky!

July 28, 2012

Hot July Days

When it's hot enough
to fry an egg,
and the July day
just seems to drag . . .

Put on your old trunks
or bathing suit,
and have some fun
without spending loot!

Pick up some tubes
for a river float,
or paddle behind
a rubber boat.

Grab a towel
and head to the crick,
by the old stump
where the rocks aren't slick.

Water wings in
the backyard pool,
filled with the hose
it's oh-so cool.

Get your sunscreen
and drive to the lake,
swim out deep
and play in the boat's wake.

Run through the pasture
to the big ditch.
By yourself?
Jump in without a stitch!

Hot July days
don't have to be dull.
Go splash around . . .
at your swimmin' hole!

August 4, 2012

Contraption

I took two shoe boxes,
and stacked them together,
then I strapped them tight,
with an old belt of leather.

I found a busted broom,
and cut off the handle,
I water-proofed the box,
with wax from a candle.

I put the handle in the side,
through a small hole,
now on the end of my stick,
I had a square bowl.

In the bottom I put,
a yogurt container,
then I poked holes in it,
like a noodle strainer.

I fastened on the net,
from my butterfly wand,
I used Goo-Gloo,
so had to wait for it to bond.

I stuck the net to the box,
with a small rat trap,
the spring was still strong,
and could definitely snap.

I reinforced the sides,
with a strand of wire,
she was a beaut,
and I couldn't wait to try her.

Now me and my faithful,
blue tick hound dog Fletcher,
can go out and use . . .
my new-fangled frog catcher!

This poem was also printed in the program for the 33rd Annual Montana Trout Unlimited Bitterroot Chapter Banquet.

August 11, 2012

Breakoff

The yawning, morning sun
ascends the sullen Sapphires.
Mist rises from the Bitterroot
smoke from liquid fires.

Against my chest waders
woodland grasses softly whisper.
Late summer's morning air
courses my lungs—getting crisper.

To my right I'm startled
by a doe and her spotted fawn
awoken by me too early
on this mid-August dawn.

Down to the river's edge
stepping around a thistle patch.
I stealthily wade on in
and loosen my trico hatch.

Slicing the air with my rod,
using a double haul cast,
my fly dead drifts the current
not too slow and not too fast.

Gently floating the fly
up to a gnarled weathered stump
a huge rainbow rose and hit
leaping with a mighty jump.

Fighting, pulling, twisting, writhing
the clear water boiled.
Lunging high, he broke the leader.
Alas, I was foiled.

Silence resumed on the river
resetting calm and peace.
Smiling inside I thought . . .
"Oh well, this is catch and release!"

August 18, 2012

Hot Dog

"It's way too hot, boy,
and I'm sorry to say
I can't leave you in the car
so sit and stay."

With big sad eyes
I watched her walk out the door,
I whined a little
and sprawled out on the floor.

The overbearing heat
caused me to drool,
I sneaked out the back
to the kiddies pool.

Right when I got outside
I was panting hard,
as I started loping
across the backyard.

I ran over
and lapped some water up,
like a brown cactus
I was one thirsty pup.

I dived right in
and began to dog paddle,
just hoping the neighbors
wouldn't tattle.

Right as I started
really feeling alive,
I heard my master's car
pull up in the drive.

She came in the front
I ran in the back door,
my clothing was dripping
all over the floor.

My wife was upset
she really flipped her lid.
"Get back outside
you're worse than a little kid!"

I guess I'm in the dog house
what a bummer.
My tale end . . .
of the dog days of summer.

August 25, 2012

A Place To Play

It was a place to play
with trucks and cars,
buckets and boats and mason jars.

We built castles with moats
and draw bridges,
high atop great mountain ridges.

We would dig deep ditches
and long tunnels,
then fill with hoses and funnels.

We'd make a bakery
that sold mud pies,
the prices varied based on size.

We'd carve out a deep pit
and fill with brew,
and dance around like witches do.

With some firecrackers
we could explode,
toy soldiers like a landmine load.

We were not rich
rather closer to poor,
and this can't be bought in a store.

Now as I'm thinking back
I'm happy still,
cause I grew up . . . with a dirt hill!

September 1, 2012

Sigh

It pains me so
and makes me sad to say
that school starts
right after Labor Day.

I'll no longer be free
without a care
I'll wake up early
brush my teeth and hair.

I'll trudge to school
in sun, rain or snow
even if I'm sick
I'll still have to go.

New pens and pencils
don't excite me much
neither new clothes,
backpacks, shoes and such.

I'd rather be outside
playing jump rope
than inside at a desk
stuck without hope.

I won't be picking
bunches of flowers
I will read books
for hours and hours.

Grammar, history
and lectures on math
right after supper
I go take my bath.

Early to bed
no more a night creature
I must be at school . . .
I'm the teacher!

September 9, 2012

Just Peachy

The harvest is here,
and it's time for peach canning.
You'll need equipment,
and some strategic planning.

Break out the water bath pot,
and the canning rack.
Set the pot to boil,
now there's no turning back!

A wide mouth funnel, lid wand,
lids and of course rings.
Then pint, or quart jars,
and those fun jar-grabber things.

You'll need a box of peaches.
Oh wait! Make that two.
The ones from Washington,
known as freestones will do.

Now boil some more water,
to blanch your peaches.
Peel them in ice water,
like the Ball book teaches.

Halve the peaches,
quarter them, or cut them smaller.
Grandma's rule?
No less than a silver dollar.

Heat up a light syrup,
of sugar and water.
Pour over the fruit,
and set the jar to totter.

Balance all of the jars,
lower them to boil.
About twenty minutes,
now repeat this toil.

Blanching, peeling, cutting,
and canning for hours.
Seems your kitchen apron,
gives you super powers!

Once all of the jars,
are covered over on top,
just sit back and listen . . .
to the lids as they pop!

September 16, 2012

I'm Gonna . . .

When schools out . . .

I'm gonna build a big fort,
with branches and sticks.

I'm gonna ride my pony,
and teach him some tricks.

I'm gonna swing on my tire,
tied to a rope.

I'm gonna ride my red wagon,
down a steep slope.

I'm gonna dam the ditch,
and make a giant flood.

I'm gonna mix the water,
with dirt to make mud.

I'm gonna shoot old pop cans,
with my pellet gun.

I'm gonna stay out 'til dark,
havin' all this fun.

But so mom won't be mad,
before any of those,

I'm gonna go upstairs . . .
and put on my play clothes.

The Big Dance

There's a big dance
being held in town tonight.
I'm going to it
and want everything right.

A very special lady
I just might meet.
I need to look sharp
and be light on my feet.

I pressed my best shirt
and got the wrinkles out.
I slicked my dark hair back
with oil of trout.

I matched my argyle socks
and shined each shoe.
They glimmered as bright
as early morning dew.

I rolled the fuzzy lint
off my blue blazer.
I shaved my face
with my electric razor.

I put a Windsor knot
in my bright red tie.
I dabbed on cologne
what a sharp lookin' guy.

I showed up on time
in very high style.
I walked inside
people started to smile.

Actually they laughed.
I showed up at the dance
I thought I was set . . .
but I forgot my pants!

September 29, 2012

Invasion

I woke this morning
to three 'copters over head.
They came without a warning
I jumped out of bed.

I opened the curtain
the air was quite foggy.
I felt for certain
this was a dream—so groggy.

But no! The 'copters were real!
In our valley?
What was the deal?
I ran out in the alley.

The sun was blood red
all of the mountains were gone!
On everyone's head
a respirator was on.

The landscape was barren
the wind blew dry and hot.
My eyes blurred while starin'
my throat burned as I thought.

I'd heard stories
of alien life invasions.
On their quarries
they'd force brain evacuations.

Had this happened now?
Had our towns been overthrown?
I thought, "Holy cow!"
"It's their mother ship's drop zone!"

I grabbed my rifle
and rushed onto the front lawn.
This was no trifle
I shouted out, "Bring it on!"

My wife called from behind,
"Is this some kind of joke!?"
"Have you lost your mind!?"
"Come in from out of the smoke."

Well to tell the truth
all because I'm no liar
though sad for the Sawtooth . . .
glad it's just a fire.

This was written while smoke from the Sawtooth fire was laying
thick in the Bitterroot Valley in September 2012.

October 6, 2012

The Apple Of My Eye

One crisp October morning
Granny took my hand
and led me to the orchard
on her plot of land.

She put her face close to mine
and said, "Listen toots.
Granny will tell you about
the best of all fruits."

She picked an apple
and with a twinkling eye
she said, "This, my dear,
makes a perfect apple pie."

"It also makes
a terrific apple cobbler
and cran-apple sauce
for your Thanksgiving gobbler."

"To make apple fritters
fry some in doughnut dough
and they're delicious in dumplings-
just so you know."

"Squeeze some in a wood press
to make sweet cider.
Strain and pasteurize for juice-
it's a bit lighter."

"Cook and mash them thick
you'll have applesauce that's nice.
For apple butter, cook slowly,
and add some spice."

"Put some caramel on one
and my heart starts throbbing
at a Halloween party
they're great for bobbing."

"Here's one for you, sweetie,
the apple of my eye."
As I rubbed it on my skirt
this was my reply:

"One apple does all of that, Granny!?
Oh my gosh!"
"Yes, my toots, one apple does . . .
it's the Macintosh!"

October 13, 2012

Autumn Leaves

The leave's fall colors
begin to show
lighting the way
for winter's soft snow.

Autumn's array
of the leaves turning
all vibrant-
like a fire burning.

The deep orange
of the mighty oak tree
mixed with yellow
a delight to see.

The majestic maple's
maroon hues
make picture perfect
countryside views.

Showing it's leaves
tall and defiant
bronze and brown
the cottonwood giant.

Red with white bark
on the river birch
a stained glass window
of nature's church.

But the aspen's color
I like best
like falling gold
on the lawn they rest.

Wish they'd stay in the tree
and just quake
'cause now I have to go . . .
out and rake!

October 20, 2012

The Tea Party

I awoke quite early
this Thursday morning
at the first sound
of the alarm clock's warning.

I popped out of bed
as fast as a shelled pea.
It was my turn to host
the mid-morning tea.

I dressed, fixed my hair
put on lipstick and blush
and prepared my parlor
with lady-like rush.

A white table cloth
with napkins freshly pressed
my finest china-
this required the best.

Mrs. Margaret
was the first to arrive.
She was always early
by no less than "five".

Making a noisy entry
was Patsy Pratt.
She talked far too much
and always brought her cat.

Mary Lou and Mary Ann
came together.
They were twin sisters-
two birds of a feather.

Into the room
charged willy-nilly Millie.
She wore funny hats
and always looked silly.

Last came our gentleman
Mr. Milt McFink.
He liked conversation
that would make you think.

In came mom, who said,
"Your cookies are ready.
What a nice tea . . .
with your dollies and teddy!"

October 27, 2012

Band Of Brigands

"Ahoy there mateys!
Avast ye land-lubbers!
It's me, Captain Cloyce
and me gang of clubbers!"

"On me left you'll see
Brian The Bone Bruiser!
He's got a choke-hold
called the silent snoozer!"

"On me right you'll meet
Jackknife Joe The Joker!
He flails around
with a red hot poker!"

"Leading the way
is Austin The Angry Ape!
With an anchor chain
he'll change your facial shape!"

"Right behind him
is Sledgehammer Sean The Stump!
Though he's quite short
he'll give your melon a thump!"

"Bringing up the rear
is Crusty One-Eyed Dean!
He'll chew you to pieces
smallest ever seen!"

"We sail the high seas
pillaging for loot!
Hand over what ye've got
or I'll have to shoot!"

"Well now, don't you darling boys
just look so sweet!
Dunk your hands in Grammy's bowl . . .
for Trick-Or-Treat!"

November 3, 2012

Stuff

There's some string in here,
some twist ties and dead batteries,
Scotch tape, rubber bands,
and a bunch of mystery keys.

Here's an old butter knife,
a nail and eight brass screws,
and look, here's a pamphlet,
for a Caribbean cruise!

There's some pliers in here,
with a rusty needle nose,
a pair of bush trimmers,
and a washer for the hose.

Here's a green pencil,
with it's eraser almost gone,
a jar with six cat-eye marbles,
and a black chess pawn.

Right here's a book of matches,
and a rumpled road map,
two thumbtacks, a yellow kazoo,
and a new mouse trap.

There's a candle in here,
to light your way in the dark,
a bag of extra shoelaces,
and a torn bookmark.

You and I could sit here longer,
and name even more,
but you probably have the same stuff . . .
in your junk drawer!

November 10, 2012

Opening Day

On the morning of
deer season's opening day
while walking to the blind
my dad had this to say:

"Back on my twelfth birthday
I got a deer rifle
for your grandma and grandpa
it was no trifle."

"I hunted with my dad
and I cherished that gun
I harvested lots of deer
except for 'the one'."

"It was my first day out
we were up before dawn
We went slowly through the woods
with our blaze orange on."

"My dad nestled me down
at the base of a tree
from that vantage point
the whole clearing I could see."

"He patted my shoulder
and then whispered, "Good luck."
He moved out of sight
to rattle me in a buck."

"Besides dad's antlers clacking
the woods were stone still
when I saw a large doe
from my spot on the hill."

"She stood tall and watchful
with her head in the sticks
I glassed her with my scope
he was a six by six!"

"All of my breath left me
my hands trembled and shook
I lost my chance
he pranced away without a look."

"And son, unlike your grandpa
I'm no yarn weaver
that was my first real bad case . . .
of buck fever!"

November 17, 2012

For What We Have

For what we have . . .
of our health.
Our possessions,
and our wealth.

For what we have . . .
of our friends.
Family?
Love without ends.

For what we have . . .
of warm clothes.
Food and drink-
can't forget those.

For what we have . . .
a soft bed.
And a roof,
over our head.

For what we have . . .
kids learning.
From teachers-
with hearts burning.

For what we have . . .
jobs to work.
And dinner out-
a nice perk.

For what we have . . .
we are free.
To speak, think, pray-
to just be.

Keeping these safe-
troops in ranks.
For what we have . . .
we give thanks.

I Forgot

I remembered,
to set my alarm clock.
I remembered,
to pair and match each sock.

I remembered,
to get myself all dressed.
I wore clean jeans
and the shirt was my best.

I remember,
I ate both my pancakes
I drank my juice
and had my frosty flakes.

I remembered,
to brush my pearly whites
I flossed and I swished
and turned off the lights.

I combed my hair
I do remember that
which I find funny
'cause I wear a hat.

I remembered,
my lunch box and my coat.
I took my field trip
permission note.

I remembered,
my math and English book.
My homework-
I know that I also took.

The role call sheet
teacher took off the shelf
but I wasn't there . . .
I forgot myself!

December 1, 2012

The Cure

Drink half-a-gallon
of room-temp orange juice.
That's according to
my great uncle Bruce.

Now if you listen to
my good friend, Dee,
you'll be guzzling
hot, licorice bark tea.

Use a poultice
of garlic and black bean.
That's a page from the book
of grandma Jean.

Eat pomegranates-
at least a dozen
and suck a lemon
says Brad, my cousin.

Boil cider vinegar
in a pot.
Inhale the fumes
while the steam is hot.

Then chew cinnamon sticks,
claims my wife.
I'm thinking to myself,
"Not on my life!"

Alternate between
hot and cold showers.
My dad insists
to do this for hours.

Sweat it out by running
around the block
my neighbor says.
I think it's just talk.

Sniff cayenne pepper
flush with salt water.
I learned that trick
from my plumber's daughter.

Always given for free
and never sold
other people's cures . . .
for the common cold!

December 8, 2012

One Thing

"Pull into the store honey
I need just one thing.
And you should come too.
Now you know it won't sting!"

"So let's grab a cart-
but it's only for my purse.
Will you push it dear?
And smile! It's not a hearse!"

"Ooh! Come over here sweetie
and be real quick!
I spotted a sale!
Now don't act like you're sick."

"Um sugar? I want to peek
at the clearance rack.
Hey just cheer up.
You're not having a heart attack!"

"Oh love! This reminds me
that our old one is broke.
Just put some pep in your step,
you're not gonna croak!"

"Sweetheart, this is five percent off!
It's gently used.
Don't moan and groan
and act like you're being abused."

"Ok darling, you push the cart
up to the front.
It's not that heavy
you don't have to strain and grunt!"

"Snookums wait! Don't go to far
here's the bargain bin!
For heaven's sake wait up front.
Shopping's not a sin!"

He stands there and listens
to the register ring
and he thinks to himself . . .
"It's never just one thing."

December 15, 2012

Office Party

'Twas the week before Christmas
and all over town
office parties like this one
were all going down.

"Hi Jessie." "Oh, Hi Katie.
I'm so glad you're here.
Stay and protect me
from the men swilling cheap beer."

"Let's stick together-
and stay away from the punch.
Jeffery from maintenance spiked it-
I have a slight hunch."

"Also, watch out for the shrimp.
I know they look nice
but they sat in the back room
without any ice."

"There goes Tiffany
throwing herself on the guys."
"She act's tipsy every year
so it's no surprise."

"There's Raymond bragging about
his yearly quota.
He talks so loud
if you ask me it's a load 'a-"

"Be sharp! Here comes Gladys
the prissy office grinch.
She'll nark on you for nothin'
and won't even flinch!"

"Look at Betsy
hog-facing the whole dessert tray!"
"Ask her—"It's my thyroid."
is what she'll always say."

"Look—it's Jason.
God's gift to women you know."
"It's creepy how he's lurking
by the mistletoe."

"I'd like to tell the boss
he doesn't own us."
"Me too. I come each year . . .
but just for my bonus!"

December 22, 2012

Her Child

Many long years ago
and rather far away,
an infant boy was born
and laid upon the hay.

His mother held her boy
up tight against her chest,
and rocked him quite gently
so her child could rest.

Her baby squirmed down gently
in his soft warm fleece,
his little mouth cooed softly
tender words of peace.

He kicked out his bare feet
and his ten tiny toes,
with those same feet
he'll spread love wherever he goes.

He reached his small hands up
for his rattling toy,
the hands that to others
would always bring great joy.

His loving mother looked down
into each bright eye,
and saw hope shining there
like the star in the sky.

His mother wrapped him up
in warm blankets piled.
The peace, love, joy and hope
of her Christmas child.

December 29, 2012

Resolutions

Every time the new year
fast approaches,
some of us become
our own life coaches.

We find problems
so we seek solutions,
in the form of
new year resolutions.

We weigh too much
so we will exercise,
and cut way back
on the milkshakes and fries.

We rush on out
and buy gym memberships,
and swear an oath against
high trans-fat chips.

As for money
we'll cut each credit card,
at least hide them-
cutting would be too hard.

No more frivolous
shopping or spending,
the days of
impulse buying are ending.

As for us smokers
we'll crush out those butts,
and slap on the patch
so we don't go nuts.

Some of us will read more
some will drink less,
some will keep their car
from being a mess.

Some will get much better
grades in school,
some will now live
by the golden rule.

These things and more
we're all going to do,
and keep these resolves . . .
for a week or two!

January 5, 2013

Have You Ever?

Ever open the fridge
going for a tasty score?
You stare blankly ahead
and then you just shut the door?

Ever go into the shop
looking for a tool?
You get lost, look around,
then feel like a fool?

Ever open up your closet
looking for some clothes?
Your mind draws a huge blank
so the closet door you close?

Ever dial a phone number
and it starts to ring?
You forget who you're calling
and hope for the machine?

Ever in the morning
open up the bathroom drawer?
You root through the stuff
but don't know what you're looking for?

Ever walk into a room
and forget why you're there?
Then you ask it out loud
to the couch and easy chair?

Ever open up a cupboard
in your own kitchen?
You don't know what you want
so you stand there head-itchin'?

Whenever this happens
to remember it for sure
just turn around and go back . . .
to wherever you were!

January 12, 2013

The Telemarketer

*ring*ring*ring*ring*
"Hello? Andersen residence."
"Good evening. This is Ben
from A-1 Common-Sense."

"Mrs. Andersen you know
the weather's colder.
Replace your furnace
it's only getting older."

"Thanks Ben, but we don't need
a furnace anymore.
You see, we recently moved
down to Ecuador."

"In that case let's talk about
your air condition."
"There's no need
we're going on a Chinese mission."

"Let me set you up
with a stainless steel wok."
"We won't have time to eat
we'll just have time to talk."

"I'd like to offer you
language tapes in high-def."
"Please understand
my husband and I are stone deaf."

"Yes ma'am, you see
the tapes are close-captioned for that."
"I forgot to mention
we're both blind as a bat."

"While you're gone
let's have your house alarmed and wired."
"There's no need.
The Andersens have both expired."

"A telemarketer?"
Mr. Andersen said.
"Yes Dear, but they won't call back . . .
I told them we're dead!"

January 19, 2013

Ice and Snow

The thick white snow
blankets the frozen ground
while it amplifies
each wintry sound.

The soft thumping
as snow sluffs off the trees
rustling branches
from the icy breeze.

The wind whispers
over the frozen pond
swirling the flakes
falling from the beyond.

The swirling snow flakes
form drifts wide and deep
and all the way down
to the creek they sweep.

Under the ice
the water swiftly flows
between the gaps
the frothy water shows.

Past the cabin
the creek winds and trickles
and from the eves
hang crystal ice cycles.

I love the winter
with it's ice and snow
that is from the warm side . . .
of the window!

January 26, 2013

Secrets

He goes to the store
but "loses" the receipt
because he bought a donut
for a small treat.

She uses mouthwash
and a scented lotion
she sneaked a smoke
because she had the notion.

He's in the pantry
for a shot of liquor
he's mighty quick
but might need a lie quicker.

She wants brownies
so cuts the edge a sliver
she's so smart and cunning
it makes her shiver.

Doc says he's got to quit
drinking so much pop
but he hides the cases
out in his work shop.

At the store she gets
an ice cream bar with nuts
then dumps the stick and wrapper
she's sure no putz.

He goes to the fridge
for a light midnight snack
he sneaks some turkey
but only from the back.

She's supposed to cut back
on candy a lot
but she hides her chocolate
in the old tea pot.

Keep your secrets safe
and don't you dare leak 'em
your spouse must never know . . .
about your "Sneak 'em"!

February 2, 2013

Groundhog Day

Five distinguished ladies
from the garden club
took a morning hike
to the Evergreen Shrub.

To see "He Who Lived
Beneath The Evergreen"
by him—with a glance-
the future could be seen.

"He won't see his shadow
he'll stay above ground."
"And that means," said Ruth,
"I can start my seed mound!"

Beth said, "He won't pop down
back into his hole
and now my clematis
can start up it's pole!"

"Speaking of poles," said Jean,
"I can start my peas.
He won't see his shadow
we've had our last freeze!"

"I'm gonna," said Sally,
"drag out my hoses.
He'll announce spring
and I'll start on my roses."

Phyllis held up her hands
and began to speak.
"I will creep to his hole
and take a quick peek."

Phyllis left the group
they all began to yak
about their plants
'til they saw her coming back.

"Well Phyllis, hurry up!
Tell us what he said!"
"It's a late spring . . .
He's not even out of bed!"

February 9, 2013

First Love

I recall my first love
back in grammar school.
I was head over heels
a love sick fool.

She wore pretty dresses
and ribbons in her hair.
I was quite mesmerized
by the perfume she'd wear.

She would pass my desk
when she'd walk up the aisle
our eyes would connect
and she would always smile.

She was quite popular
the center of each group
and her penmanship had
a swirly loop-the-loop.

Sometimes I'd play dumb
so she'd help me with my math.
Mom didn't understand
why now I'd take a bath.

Her lilting laughter
was like music to my ears.
As February approached
I suppressed my fears.

I had to be brave
to make her my valentine.
I'm sad to report though
that she was never mine.

I expressed my love,
she pointed out one feature.
We couldn't be valentines . . .
she was my teacher!

Characters

"Arrgh matey!" he cried
and snarled a sneer.
Closing one eye,
"I'll cut ya' ear to ear!"

"I'm a damsel
distraught and in distress!"
She pouts, bats her eyes
and smoothes out her dress.

He takes off his shirt
and flexes his arms.
"Yes, I'm buff ladies
suave, and full of charms."

Stretching her eyes
she twists her bottom lip.
"I have just arrived
from the mother ship!"

"Listen up partner
you low down skunk—draw!"
He points his finger guns
and spits some chaw.

She musses her hair
where the fleas all thrive.
With wild eyes
"I'm off to dumpster dive!"

He sucks in his cheeks
and pastes his hair back.
"Good day sir,
I've warmed up the Cadillac."

She pulls a towel down
over her ears.
Wrinkling her face
"Come to Granny my dears!"

Be who you'd like!
Go to far off places!
Just sit at the mirror . . .
and make faces!

February 23, 2013

Pot Luck

It was Saturday night
at Community Hall
for the city wide pot luck
and Late Winter Ball.

Some folks came for dancing
others came for the food
on the back wall sat two guys-
but not to be rude.

It was a dad and young son
learning a lesson
about how pot lucking
is much about guessin'.

"Son, here come the twins.
Sisters Bobbi and Betty
between the two
they make a squishy spaghetti."

"Coming through the door
is Marilyn Macintosh
she always brings
her beefy rice and bean goulash."

"Jean Johnson's scalloped potatoes
are hard and cold.
Sue Ann's 'fresh' dinner rolls
are store bought and day old."

"Miss Martha's noodle salad
has mayo and nuts,
raisins and pretzels
that look like cigarette butts."

"There's mushy meatballs,
thick chili and boiling soups.
And grey mystery meat
whispered about in groups."

"Burnt brownies, crummy cookies,
bars that taste like fish.
Giddy ladies asking
if you tried their hot dish."

"Dad, I get 'pot'
but is 'luck' if the food don't stick?"
"No, Eli, the luck comes in . . .
if you don't get sick!"

March 2, 2013

Good News

This morning I stepped out
for the daily news
I searched for signs of spring-
her small, subtle clues.

My breath didn't billow
like a puff of steam
with each invisible breath-
of spring I dream.

The sun is earlier
with his morning rays
I yearned in the sunlight-
for spring's warmer days.

I cast a quick glance up
at the mountain side
with hopes of spring-
I see the snowline subside.

There are small green tips
in the dry flower beds
tulips promising spring-
with their peeking heads.

I see the water
in Toby Kitty's dish
it is unfrozen-
will spring grant me my wish?

I grabbed my paper
my heart started throbbin'
on the lawn—spring . . .
showing off her first robin!

BONUS POEMS

Brother

We play in the mud
and roll in the dirt,
throw rocks at each other
even though it will hurt.

We fish in ponds
and wade in cricks.
We hit each other
with great big sticks.

We catch salamanders
and capture frogs.
We push each other
off of hollow logs.

We play ball
with bats and gloves
and settle disputes
with pushes and shoves.

We fly kites
and we race cars
and give each other
cuts and scars.

But I'd rather spend time
with no other.
There's just something great . . .
about my brother!

Zing-A-Ma-Twirl

I asked my dad
if I could have a bike.
He said, "Not yet.
You're just a little tyke."

So I asked him
for a new swing.
"Oh not yet.
You're still a little thing."

When I told him
that my brother did,
he said, "Well sorry.
You're still a little kid."

Well I have muscles
and I have brains
so I gathered my brother's
broken trains.

I pulled off the wheels
and took out the gears.
He wouldn't notice
'cause he hasn't used them in years.

I got the pedals and chain
off his busted bike.
I got the streamers too
and the horn that I like.

I got the handle and axles
from his wagon that's rusty.
I grabbed the seat from his trike
even though it was dusty.

I used some of the springs
from his old trampoline.
There were holes in it
bigger than you'd ever seen.

I scrounged up some boards,
nails and screws from my dad's shop.
Then some rope, wire
and the handle of an old mop.

I cut with the saw
and nailed with the hammer.
Screwed with the driver
and made quite a clamor.

I worked all afternoon
and into the night.
And when it was done
what a beautiful sight!

Next day as I drove through the yard,
dad said, "What'cha got there?
It looks like it's been made
with nothing but parts that were spare."

"Well that's the truth daddy,
It's my zing-a-ma-twirl!
I made it by myself . . .
not bad for a little girl!"

Guido

Guido has this one pair
they're a lovely lime green
and he wore his red pair
in a picture with the queen!

He likes his black ones
with the stripe of yellow
and when he wears them
he's one happy fellow!

When you stare at his purple ones
with the little white dots
even after you look away
you still see the spots!

When he lost his pink ones
he was oh so sad.
But his bright orange ones?
He thinks they're simply rad!

The white ones are for home
but his pair of dark brown
he always, always wears those
when he goes downtown!

You see, the brown ones,
match his almondy eyes
but none of Guido's Speedos . . .
match his large size!

Alarm

*BEEP*BEEP*BEEP*BEEP*

The alarm clock screams.
"I'm awake . . ."
I mumble from my dreams.

*BEEP*BEEP*BEEP*BEEP*

I reach over and hit snooze.
I don't care if I'm late
I only have my job to lose.

*BEEP*BEEP*BEEP*BEEP*

I'm startled mid-snore.
That darn alarm
I can no longer ignore.

*BEEP*BEEP*BEEP*BEEP*

Okay! I'm up! I'm up!
Now will you please point the way . . .
to my coffee cup.

Serious 66

I love to titter
I love to laugh.
I love to guffaw
and I love to gaff.

I love to chuckle
I love to chortle.
Sometimes I laugh so hard
I start to snortle.

Giggling is great fun
and snickering too.
Once I laughed so long
that I turned blue.

"Your laughing too much!"
mom and dad would preach.
"And at school too!
Your teacher can't teach!"

"Don't laugh at the table!
Don't laugh in the bath!
Don't laugh in Science, History,
English or Math!"

"Don't laugh while I'm driving
or when I'm on the phone!
If you wanna laugh
do it when you're alone!"

"If you ever get a job
you can't laugh there!
Your constant laughing
is more than I can bear!"

"Stop all that laughing
while I'm talking to you!
We're going to the doctor
that's what we'll do!"

The doctor said,
"Your boy's really in a fix."
Then he gave me a shot . . .
of Serious 66.

Now I don't laugh
I just sit and stare off
and hope that one day . . .
this medicine will wear off.